BOOK ANALYSIS

By Joanna Glum

Death of a Salesman

BY ARTHUR MILLER

Bright
≡**Summaries**.com

Shed new light
on your favorite books with

Bright
≡Summaries.com

www.brightsummaries.com

ARTHUR MILLER	**9**
DEATH OF A SALESMAN	**13**
SUMMARY	**17**

Act 1: Biff is Home
Act 2: An Appointment
Requiem: "We're free."

CHARACTER STUDY	**29**

Willy Loman
Linda Loman
Biff Loman
Happy Loman
Charley
Bernard
Uncle Ben
The Woman
Howard Wagner

ANALYSIS	**41**

The American Dream, modernity and its context
Immateriality in the theatrical space
Growing up and concepts of masculinity

FURTHER REFLECTION	**49**
FURTHER READING	**53**

ARTHUR MILLER

AMERICAN PLAYWRIGHT

- **Born in Harlem, New York City in 1915.**
- **Died in Roxbury, Connecticut in 2005.**
- **Notable works:**
  - *All My Sons* (1947), play
  - *The Crucible* (1953), play
  - *A View from the Bridge* (1955, revised 1956), play

Arthur Miller is one of the most celebrated figures in the world of 20th century drama, and his four major works remain a part of the theatrical canon across the globe. Born into a modestly wealthy home in New York, Miller supported himself early in his career with work writing radio plays and at other menial jobs; he was in his early 30s before he reached his current level of renown with the play *All My Sons*. His life was marked by a certain degree of celebrity, having been called to testify before the House of Un-American Activities at the height of McCarthyism and having been married tumultuously to Marilyn

Monroe (American actress, 1926-1962), with the troubles that plagued their relationship being chronicled in the 1967 play *The Price*.

Despite having written only 17 plays throughout his career, none of which matched the success of his early, now canonical works, Miller enjoyed a long and multi-faceted career as an essayist, short story writer, and screenwriter. Throughout his life, Miller's works never strayed far from the concerns that first brought him to the stage: he continued to question growing tides of nationalism, xenophobia, and modernization in his postwar country, and his eye remained ever-fixed on the average person fighting for a small, dignified life even in worlds of chaos.

DEATH OF A SALESMAN

1949 RECIPIENT OF THE PULITZER PRIZE FOR DRAMA

- **Genre:** play (tragedy)
- **Reference edition:** Miller, A. (2011) *Death of a Salesman*. London: Pearson Longham.
- **1st edition:** 1949
- **Themes:** masculinity, maturity and adulthood, modernity, capitalism and materialism

Regarded as one of the finest pieces of 20th-century American drama (along with *A Streetcar Named Desire* [1947] by Tennessee Williams [American playwright, 1911-1983] and *A Long Day's Journey into Night* [1956] by Eugene O'Neill [American playwright, 1888-1953]), Miller's play is an elegy for the impossible American Dream and the common man who is crushed in its pursuit. Produced at a time of sweeping societal change in a post-war America, *Death of a Salesman* shares with its dramatic cousins a lament for the Old Way of Life that never can be again, and similarly follows the seemingly inevitable demise of a tragic hero whose tragic flaw proves to be an adherence to the promise of a past that no longer exists (if it ever did).

Miller's work is distinguished by its characteristic theatrical ephemerality: the Lomans' house always symbolically functions as more than just the house, with reality merely acting as an ineffable gateway into the imagined, and Willy's dreams and expectations are just as fleeting and intangible. Miller's creation of a rich tapestry of characters and the focus on the interiority of his protagonist through formalistically poetic means continues to influence the development of modern American drama.

SUMMARY

ACT 1: BIFF IS HOME

Willy Loman arrives home from an aborted work trip, exhausted, having lost himself in his thoughts on the road. His wife, Linda, suggests that he ask for work near their New York home while Willy laments the passing of his old boss Wagner and the difficulties in dealing with Howard, Wagner's son and Willy's new, younger boss.

The couple discuss their eldest son Biff's return to New York, with Willy both accusing his boy of being lazy and yet not lazy, merely lost. Upstairs, Happy, the Loman's younger son, reveals to his brother that their father has begun to talk to himself, usually about Biff.

The brothers discuss their respective lives, Biff saying that he has had a series of jobs as a farmhand and offering to take his brother back out West on his return. Happy, however, insists that he will work his way up at his current company, where he now beds executives' wives for the thrill of the power. Biff reveals that he has a plan to ask an old acquaintance, Bill Oliver, for a small loan so that he might be able to start a ranch of his own.

Meanwhile, downstairs, Willy descends into the first of many hallucinations of a remembered past, on this occasion imagining a time when Biff and Happy were boys. Willy fondly remembers how Biff fixed their Chevy and was a well-liked captain of the football team. Willy remarks that while the neighbour Charley's son, Bernard, is intelligent, he is not well-liked – nor is his father. Willy regales the boys with tales from his successful sales trip in New England, commenting that he has a wealth of friends in Boston.

In the hallucination, Linda goes over sums from Willy's paycheque, counting the bills for appliance purchases and repairs. Willy grows increasingly distressed and divulges to Linda his belief that people laugh at him because he talks too much, whereas Charley, he believes, is respected. Meanwhile, Willy's hallucination splits, and the sound and image of a laughing Woman fades into the scene as Willy discusses how hard it is to be on the road. Willy moves into this part of the hallucination, giving The Woman a new pair of silk stockings; in return, she promises to get him right to the buyers, and it becomes clear they have been carrying on an affair in Boston.

Returning to his former hallucination, Willy furiously admonishes Linda for darning her socks as Bernard enters, pestering Biff to study with him for fear that he will fail his math class. Willy angrily rebuffs Bernard, asserting that Biff needs nothing.

Willy then comes out of his reverie. Happy heads downstairs and soothes Willy, who now laments that he could have been striking it rich with his brother Ben in Alaska. Charley, the neighbour, arrives and asks to play cards with Willy. Though the game is amiable at first, Willy calls Charley disgusting, fading again into a hallucination – this time of his brother, Ben. He asks Ben when their mother died, and as his delusion blends with reality, Charley grows increasingly confused and Willy increasingly infuriated, claiming that Charley is not a 'real man'. He imagines the time Ben visited his family in New York, detailing the trip to Africa that made him rich, with Willy asking his brother about their father in order to tell his sons what kind of stock they come from. Willy flatters Biff while ignoring Happy's joyful claim that he has lost weight.

Willy is broken out of his reverie by Linda as the boys come downstairs. Biff wonders how long Willy has been that bad, and Linda reveals that the hallucinating gets worse when Biff comes home. She wishes that father and son could soothe the animosity between them, and says if Biff is to love her, he must love his father as well. Biff claims Charley is a better man in that he would not "spew [...] vomit from his mind" (p. 44) in his family's house, but Linda says even a small man can get as exhausted as a big man.

She divulges that Willy has lost his salary at the company and has been taking 50 dollars a week from Happy, pretending it is his pay. Biff promises that he will return to the city he hates, earn money for the family, live in their house, and take care of everything, but that he will not speak to Willy.

His mother reveals that she suspects that Willy has tried to kill himself. Biff says he will try making it in business for the family, but Happy sharply says that Biff has to learn to play the game, as some in business world think Biff is crazy – for Biff does whistle in the elevator.

Willy re-enters and asks who thinks he is crazy. He begins to insult Biff, claiming that his son never grew up and that Bernard would certainly never whistle in elevators. Happy quells the growing argument by saying that Biff intends to ask Bill Oliver for a loan to start a family business in sporting goods. Willy's demeanour changes instantly, and Biff also seems pleased by the idea of going into business with his brother.

Willy bombards Biff with advice about how to conduct himself in the meeting, eventually contradicting himself. Throughout, he tells Linda to stop interrupting, and Biff grows increasingly angry with his father for yelling at his mother. Willy storms out of the room.

The act ends with Biff acquiescing by saying good night to his father, though Willy again bulldozes the conversation, prompting Linda to ask Willy why Biff hates him. Willy speaks fondly of how Biff stood once like a young god on the football field, and he goes to bed looking at the moonlight between the buildings, saying everything will be alright in the morning. Before going to bed, Biff removes the piece of rubber coiling from behind the furnace.

ACT 2: AN APPOINTMENT

The next morning Willy wakes up in a pleasant mood which sours after he hears about the bills he has to pay to fix the refrigerator. Linda encourages him, saying that they are almost done paying off their mortgage, and reminds him to ask Howard for an advance and a New York position. Linda tells Willy that his sons are treating him to a steak dinner that night, and he leaves buoyed. On a call to Biff, Linda trembles with joy at the prospect of the boys saving their father's life.

At the office, Willy's boss, Howard, plugs in a recorder and makes Willy listen to his family whistling. Though Willy reminisces about an old salesman who worked well into his 80s and died the "death of a salesman" (p. 160) on the road, he himself is practically unknown on the road now and wants to work in New York. Instead, Howard brushes him off, fires him, and tells him to rest.

Willy reacts poorly, and after Howard leaves him to cool off in the office, Willy has a vision of Ben. His brother asks Willy to join him in Alaska, and while Willy seems to want to, Linda encourages him to remain firm in his choice to be a salesman. Ben leaves, and Willy says they will make their life in New York. This hallucination fades into one of Biff before his big game at Ebbots Field, and Willy says everything rides on that day. Before fading out of his hallucination, Charley in the memory asks Willy when he will ever grow up.

Howard's office bleeds into present-day Charley's office, where Willy meets Bernard, who is doing well for himself as a lawyer. Willy breaks down in an earnest moment and asks why Biff never cut in like Bernard. Bernard retorts by asking Willy why Biff did not complete the one summer course he needed to graduate after his math teacher flunked him in high school, perhaps implicating Willy in the decision. However, Willy says he pleaded with Biff to go and has been wondering for 15 years why Biff did not go. Bernard wonders if Biff had gone up to Boston to visit Willy afterwards, and Willy becomes irate. Charley enters, and Willy asks for 50 dollars to cover bills and then enough to pay insurance. Charley instead offers him a job, but Willy does not take him up on it. Charley says he knows that Willy has been jealous of him his whole life and gives him money to cover his full insurance anyway. Willy remarks that a man is worth more dead than alive, asks Charley to say sorry to Bernard for him, and says Charley is his only real friend.

The setting bleeds into the bar, where Happy lies wildly to hit on a woman while waiting for his brother. Biff arrives and reveals that Oliver did not even recognize him and that he walked out after stealing Oliver's fountain pen. Happy asks Biff to lie about the deal to Willy to keep him happy. Willy arrives, and though Happy tries to maintain a lie, and though Willy reveals he was fired, Biff cannot do anything but tell the truth about his failure. Willy descends into a sharp hallucination that crosses the line of the bar, and as the men continue speaking, Willy imagines young Bernard telling Linda that Biff has failed math. Willy eventually runs out of the bar and Biff reproaches Happy for not helping Willy out more. Meanwhile, The Woman has begun to enter the remembered scene, and it eventually dominates the stage, revealing that young Biff indeed took a train up to Boston and walked in on his father in his hotel room. While Willy made The Woman hide in the bathroom, she revealed herself, and all at once Biff's request for his father to intervene on his behalf with his math teacher was lost and so was Biff. Willy is brought out of his delusion by the waiter at the restaurant to find that his sons have left with the woman Happy had been hitting on. Willy asks the waiter where he can buy some seeds.

Back at home, Linda is distraught and condemns the boys for not caring about whether Willy lives or dies. Happy tries to maintain that they did not leave their father, but Biff cuts him off and takes the abuse his mother directs at him, not objecting when she calls him a louse, and asking merely to speak to Willy. It is revealed that he is in their backyard, planting seeds and talking once again to his hallucination of Ben, this time telling his brother his plans for a grand funeral that will show others just how important he was. Ben says he will consider the proposition, and Biff enters the space to say goodbye to Willy before leaving New York the next day.

In a final confrontation, Biff forcibly tells Willy that he does not want to be something he is not, that neither of them are anything more than a dime a dozen, that he wants to go back to the small things he loves, and that it is nobody's fault. He breaks down in his father's arms and runs to bed. Willy is overwhelmed, saying that Biff really loves him. Linda begs Willy to go to bed, but he asks for just a minute, and in a final hallucination, he rejoices that 20 000 dollars (now abundantly clear to be his life insurance) will set up Biff well. Willy speeds off in his car. The music indicates that he has died, and the family, along with Charley and Bernard, re-emerge dressed for a funeral.

REQUIEM: "WE'RE FREE."

At the grave, Linda wonders where all the people were for Willy's funeral. Happy is distraught. Biff is calm, and says Willy never knew who he was, and that was the reason for his demise. Biff offers Happy the chance to return with him to the West, but Happy obstinately refuses, claiming that he will win the fight his father began, trying to be number one in the city. He leaves, and Linda, at first unable to cry at her husband's grave, finally breaks down, saying they have finally paid off their house and are "free" (p. 112).

CHARACTER STUDY

WILLY LOMAN

Willy Loman is a 20th-century 'every man' working American. When he enters the scene, he is said to be, "dressed quietly" (p. 8). Throughout the play, Willy's despair is proven to be rooted in just this kind of averageness: though striving to be a great man, thinking up elaborate means by which to achieve success, Willy is proven to be washed-up in his old age and in his new world. While he is sometimes a gentle-mannered and loving man, his life's failures have accumulated to create the fuel for a violent bitterness, often indirectly weaponized against his submissive wife, Linda, and directly aimed at his son, Biff. This father-son relationship provides the foundation for understanding the tragic fall of both men from their presupposed heights, and while Biff has been able to move on with his life, Willy cannot and remains rooted in an attempt to relive (and ostensibly correct) history.

Willy's struggle is the crux of the show, and his tragic downfall is precipitated by his imagination. Willy imagines that both anything is possible – that the American Dream is achievable – and also that his memories are his reality. Both aspects of 'imagining' contribute to Willy's fatal paranoia and depression. However, the themes throughout the show suggest that Willy's true *hamartia* (a literary term meaning 'fatal flaw') is that he never fully knew himself. As Willy says to his brother Ben in one flashback, "I still feel – kind of temporary about myself" (p. 40), and he constantly tries to escape the feeling that he has never grown up by attempting to live up to other people's definitions of what it means to be a "real man" (*ibid.*). As such, his ultimate goal is one of self-definition; similarly, his mistake was seeking to define himself by his work and his success as opposed to something more organic, as suggested by Biff's final assertion.

LINDA LOMAN

Linda Loman is both the member of the family with the smallest role and the last word. Miller endows her with "an iron repression [...] to Willy's behaviour" (p. 8), asserting that she loves him in spite of his cruel unpredictability because, ultimately, she shares the same "longings" (*ibid.*) as him, though without his "temperament" (*ibid.*). As such, Linda's character construction runs parallel to the female characters in many of Miller's plays: they are either the catalyst to or the crutch for the male protagonist's turmoil. Linda is Willy's crutch, and it is clear that without her unconditional care, he might have collapsed sooner than he had.

Linda in many ways compels Biff's actions against his father in defence of his mother; we see this both in the present of the play, where at the end of Act 1 Biff attacks his father for telling Linda to shut up, and in the more foundational flashbacks, where Biff's collapse is precipitated by his father's infidelity towards his mother. This highlights the functional role Linda plays within the text: it is through Linda's lists and revelations that the audience learns necessary pieces of expository information (such as Willy's attempted suicides and the state of the Lomans' economic affairs), and this information further fuels the internal and interpersonal struggles of the Loman men.

Linda's final monologue at her husband's grave suggests that her sense of freedom stems in greater part from her husband's passing than the house's newfound stability, and as she is escorted to and from the grave by Charley, it is suggested that while she will remain stable, Willy's death has robbed her of both her husband and the desperate longings she shared with him, which were at once a blessing and a burden to them both.

BIFF LOMAN

Biff provides the dramatic counterpoint to Willy, and their relationship drives the conflict of the play.

Once a hometown hero, the captain of the football team poised to turn his humble roots into success with athletic scholarships to leading universities, Biff's life has since been defined by a series of failures after a mysterious breakdown during his senior year of high school. Though he had the opportunity to make up his failed math course, Biff's fateful trip to visit Willy in Boston and subsequent discovery of his father's infidelity precipitated a life removed from the kind of success Willy had envisioned for his son.

His disillusionment, then, arrives when Willy's never does. Though Willy's life is full of theatrical and thematic illusions, his refusal to confront them is seen to be the cause of his downfall. Biff's failure, on the other hand, is proven to be a kind of success whereby Biff is able to forge a reality of his own after being confronted with the harsh reality of his father's imperfections, though not without difficulty.

Biff thematically complements his Uncle Ben as a man whose life is made (or in the process of being made) outside of the rat race of New York City, in which Willy is so deeply invested. The rift between father and son can be boiled down to an ideological difference in the means by which they each validate and seek their identity: Biff, being unperturbed by an existence outside of the esteem and renown of the big city, provides consternation for his father, whose life is founded on the idea that his identity should be created and validated by the very city that is crushing it.

HAPPY LOMAN

Happy lives up to his name, positioning himself as the Loman family's talisman of positivity.

He has reached a moderate level of success in his business world (though not as much as he purports), but he squanders his money on philandering and women. In Biff's absence, Happy has taken over as a kind of family caregiver, but it is clear that he has never received the kind of attention he has desired. In fact, his claim that he has "more in [his] pinky finger than [his boss]'s got in his head" (p. 18) appears to echo a broader sentiment that has been following him since his childhood, when he would try to get Willy's attention by showing him how much weight he had lost, but was merely rejected because of his father's focus on Biff's accomplishments.

When looking at the play in terms of Greek Tragedy, in which the perpetuation of a curse condemns generations within one family, Happy seems to take up his father's tragic mantle by the end of the play. His stubborn refusal to head West with his brother echoes Willy's refusal to move away with his own brother Ben, and in this comparative light, Happy's persistent happiness, which is buoyed by lies told to those closest to him, seems to echo his father's own propensity to devolve into hallucination of an imagined 'better' or 'other' life.

CHARLEY

The Lomans' pragmatic neighbour Charley finds the very success for which Willy searches by virtue of the fact, seemingly, that he does not himself care about finding it at all. "All you've got is what you can sell" he proclaims to Willy (p. 76), who scorns Charley for having achieved success without, ostensibly, having the virtues of a 'well-liked' personality that Willy holds in such high esteem.

Charley and Willy find themselves caught in a rhetorical battle about 'growing up', with Willy claiming that Charley does not possess the qualities of a 'real man', while Charley asks Willy when he will 'grow up' by leaving behind his dream-filled notions of illustrious success. Though their relationship is marked by a degree of acrimony, largely due to Willy's jealousy of Charley and his refusal to accept the generosity of his neighbour, Willy asserts that Charley is his only real friend, and it is clear that Charley believes him.

BERNARD

Like his father Charley, Bernard functions as a foil to Biff and an expositional tool deployed by Miller to reveal the inciting incident and the consequences that surround it. Studious but often seen in knickers as a young man, Bernard is wholly dismissed by Willy for not being well-liked like Biff; however, as an adult Bernard achieves the kind of social-climbing stature through his position as a lawyer that Willy had presumably hoped his own son would achieve. Willy had also desired this kind of success for himself, and having the model family of the American Dream live next door serves only to exacerbate Willy's feelings of failure.

UNCLE BEN

Uncle Ben is the imagined ideal of the American success story. He is said to have travelled south from Alaska into Africa, where he found himself in the jungle and re-emerged a man made rich by diamonds. "The jungle is dark but full of diamonds" he tells his brother (p. 106), and Ben acts as a source of darkness throughout the play, cursing Willy through either remembered or purely imagined examples of a life that could have been, but never was.

THE WOMAN

The Woman is a purely functional character whose affair with Willy triggers the catastrophe at the heart of the play. That she continues to promise Willy inside access to the salesmen in the office she works in, and yet never seems to deliver on that promise, serves to further symbolize the ways in which Willy's dreams of success are held tantalizingly out in front of him but are never realised – and, in fact, may never have even existed in the first place. Willy's downfall is therefore due in part to his susceptibility to this seduction and rejection of reality. The Woman may also act as a foil for Linda who, in this case, might represent the 'real' – a wife who mends the holes in her stockings and does not attempt to fulfil a glamorous role, all while providing tangible support for Willy.

HOWARD WAGNER

Willy's new boss Howard represents everything that modernity brings to bear on the old world. With no time for the older generation, even those who have dedicated their lives to a company, Howard maintains standards of efficiency that, though not malicious, are certainly not focused on the human behind the worker. His casual brush-off of Willy in the latter's most desperate moment reads as a gesture of what the new world might offer – an assessment that some people are simply dispensable.

ANALYSIS

THE AMERICAN DREAM, MODERNITY AND ITS CONTEXT

The junkyard

"I'm always in a race with the junkyard," Willy claims of his struggle to maintain bills on buying, repairing, and maintaining his household appliances (p. 57). As the home is the locus of the play, its contents hold a great symbolic weight, and Miller fills the space with the products of a modern mid-20th-century house.

Miller wrote the play in the period just after World War II, when the United States was riding on a boom of economic production that would soon lead to the 'fabulous 50s', a time marked by the rise of a consumerist lifestyle as the apotheosis of achieving the American Dream. Images advertised to the country held the promise of two cars per house, a white picket fence, and Campbell's Soup for everyone. Miller's world, like the Loman family's world, is indelibly tied to the 'stuff' that supports the imagery of a successful, happy family.

However, the Lomans' appliances are always on the verge of breaking. That which was once new is shown to be on the brink of disrepair in a symbolic reflection not only of Willy's loss of efficacy in his world but also of the ways in which even the possibilities offered by modernity are insufficient to make society's dreams of prosperity a reality. Willy's lamentation provides an immediate link between his economic situation and his personal situation in that, because he can no longer be a functional cog in the economic framework of a growing capitalist society, he himself is in a race against time and being scrapped. The disposal of the less efficient members of society is further brought into relief during Willy's interactions with younger characters who live robust lives, as seen in his interactions with Howard and Bernard, which will be discussed in further detail later.

A piece of fruit

Willy's most passionate plea is delivered at a moment when he must confront the ways in which he and his lifestyle have become obsolete in the fast-moving, modern world. "You can't eat the orange and throw the peel away – a man is not a piece of fruit!" he says (p. 64). This refusal to be dehumanized in the context of a mechanized and capitalist world is at the heart of Willy's cognitive dissonance – even while clearly articulating the effects of modernization on the workforce, Willy is never able to identify and name it as such.

IMMATERIALITY IN THE THEATRICAL SPACE

In his opening stage direction, Miller indicates of the Loman house that "an air of a dream clings to the place, a dream rising out of reality" (p. 7). This reality is marked by the image of the Loman home standing solitary in a jungle of high-rises. This, of course, symbolically reflects the ways in which Willy Loman stands alone, the memory of an old way of life in a rapidly changing landscape of modernity. However, Miller leverages the relationship of his formal structuring of theatrical space to the thematic content of the play, as his choices both to break with the sense of linear theatrical time through the device of

Willy's hallucinations and to blur the boundaries of theatrical space point to an inability to ever ground oneself in the 'real'.

The Loman house is transparent, and yet the characters observe its invisible partitions, creating a viable theatrical model of a 'real' house. However, the moment that Willy descends into hallucination and the boundaries of the home are blurred, the transparency of the home is brought into sharp relief, and as a viewer you are forced to confront that this 'home' is in fact built and kept on nothing. The tenuous reality of this space reflects two things: Willy's inability to remain rooted in his world as a result of his mental collapse, and the idea that the foundation of his aspirations, the promise of the American Dream, is as ineffable as the home itself. That the most material product in the most material age is, in fact, immaterial in the theatrical context serves to highlight Miller's thematic focus.

Furthermore, this immaterial house relates to the presence of hallucinations, which sometimes double as ghosts. Willy is surrounded by the shadows of figures that perhaps once existed but have since been stolen from him; he yet returns to them in hopes that they might point his way to the future. Willy exists in a kind of purgatory, and his house that is both a house and not a house, filled with people who are both people and hallucinations, further imprisons Willy in this purgatory between his past and the unliveable present that eventually delivers him unto his death.

GROWING UP AND CONCEPTS OF MASCULINITY

"Maybe that's my trouble. I'm like a boy," Biff tells his brother at the start of the play (p. 17). The journey taken, however, proves that the characteristics that Biff assumes make him boy-like (his lack of a steady job and his own house) are actually products of a self-actualized manhood. Biff has forged his own identity, and so at the end of the play escapes alive, so to speak. The preoccupation with what constitutes a man, however, defines much of Willy's internal strife. His request of his brother Ben to regale him with stories of their father is a request to reaffirm the imagistic ideal of manhood that Willy had built up in his head and against whose standard he holds himself. His pursuit of the image of manhood and maturity is proven to be that which prevents him from ever truly pursuing his own identity.

Miller utilizes a few choice stage directions to indicate that both Charley and his son Bernard wear knickers in the present and in the hallucinations of the past. Willy fixates on these details, proclaiming that neither of his neighbours is a man, and Miller theatrically presents them in the clothes worn, typically, by boys. Willy is focused, then, on the image of a man. This highlights the ways in which his futile pursuit of success in the business world is a pursuit of an external recognition and validation from his community, seen clearly in his preoccupation with the number of attendees at his eventual funeral.

The use of the epithet "kid" to describe Willy – employed both by Howard Wagner and Bernard in the crucial Act 2 – serves to diminish Willy's self-image as a man of some substance. Given that both Howard and Bernard are much younger than Willy, and in fact were once kids under Willy's supervision, his struggle to claim a title of manhood reflects a greater struggle in the context of modernity casting off those elder members of society who simply cannot keep up in the new, fast-paced economy.

FURTHER REFLECTION

SOME QUESTIONS TO THINK ABOUT...

- Consider the Wagner family further. What does Miller seem to indicate with his brief portrayal of the young family in the record played in Howard's office?
- How does reading *A Death of a Salesman* in conjunction with its cousin, *A Streetcar Named Desire*, elucidate or bring into relief thematic similarities in the two works? How does the way Miller chooses to tackle the subject at hand differ from Williams', and how might you say this moulds the particular vision of the 'future' that the author holds?
- Consider the soundscape that Miller creates throughout the play. How does the punctuation of the flute music serve the plot, the characterization of Willy, and the thematic content discussed above?
- Theatre is a living art. Consider both contemporary and past productions of *Death of a*

Salesman. How has the interpretation of the play changed or not changed in its articulation onstage? Do certain productions seek to highlight some themes or motifs above others? If so, why might that be?
- Is Ben Willy's angel or Willy's demon? In other words, how can we read his character when he is conjured purely by Willy's fallible memory and/or hallucination? Are there any indications that Ben might be less of a success or hero than Willy seems to believe?
- How might you characterize the treatment of women in the play? Biff, Ben, Bernard, and Charley notably are without the company of women; how might you then understand the relationship between fantasy and reality in the context of men and women?
- What does Miller suggest by having Linda walk to Willy's funeral arm-in-arm with Charley?
- Read again the passage in which Bernard discusses the aftermath of Biff's trip to Boston. What is the relationship between the two men, especially when they were boys?

*We want to hear from you!
Leave a comment on your online library
and share your favourite books on social media!*

FURTHER READING

REFERENCE EDITION

- Miller, A. (2011) *Death of a Salesman: Longman Study Edition*. London: Pearson Longman.

REFERENCE STUDIES

- Bloom, H. (2009) *Tennessee Williams, Updated Edition*. New York: Infobase Publishing.

- Isherwood, C. and McKinley, J. (2005) Arthur Miller, Legendary American Playwright, Is Dead. *The New York Times*. [Online]. [Accessed 21 November 2018]. Available from: <https://www.nytimes.com/2005/02/11/theater/arthur-miller-legendary-american-playwright-is-dead.html>

- Mason, J. D. (2014) Arthur Miller: A Radical Politics of the Soul. *The Oxford Handbook of American Drama*. [Online]. Accessed 7 November 2018. Available from: <http://www.oxfordhandbooks.com/view/10.1093/oxfordhb/9780199731497.001.0001/oxfordhb-9780199731497-e-016>

- Richards, J., Nathans, H. and Mason, J. (2014) Arthur Miller. *The Oxford Handbook of American Drama*. Oxford: Oxford University Press.

ADDITIONAL SOURCES

- Miller, A. (2012) *Timebends: A Life*. London: Bloomsbury.

ADAPTATIONS

- *Death of a Salesman*. (1951) [Film]. László Benedek. Dir. United States: Colombia Pictures.
- *Death of a Salesman*. (1985) [Television film]. Volker Schlöndorff. Dir. United States: Punch Productions/Roxbury Productions.

Bright≡Summaries.com

BOOK ANALYSIS

More guides to rediscover your love of literature

Animal Farm by George Orwell

The Stranger by Albert Camus

Harry Potter and the Sorcerer's Stone by J.K. Rowling

The Silence of the Sea by Vercors

Antigone by Jean Anouilh

The Flowers of Evil by Baudelaire

www.brightsummaries.com

Although the editor makes every effort to
verify the accuracy of the information published,
BrightSummaries.com accepts no responsibility for
the content of this book.

© BrightSummaries.com, 2019. All rights reserved.

www.brightsummaries.com

Ebook EAN: 9782808015691

Paperback EAN: 9782808015707

Legal Deposit: D/2018/12603/543

Cover: © Primento

Digital conception by Primento, the digital partner of publishers.

Printed in Great Britain
by Amazon